Advance Praise for
The Place the Spiders Waved

The Place the Spiders Waved finds Griffith at her cogitative best, using achingly beautiful language to delve into the people and places that raised her. Centered around a childhood on the Esperanza Ranch, Griffith's triumphant collection reminds us that we are echoes of our own experiences-- webs of passions and perspectives, of lessons learned and innocence lost.

With pastoral reverence, Griffith offers liturgy for the land. How, like a mother, it can be gentle or rough in its teaching. Or how truth and thorn scrub can be equally difficult to navigate.

Craftwise, Griffith is at her finest. She is Chopin tinkering with keys. Blank verse and triptychs, odes and elegies, anthropomorphic here and connecting narratives there – Griffith plays the right note on every page. This is a collection I will return to time and again with grateful longing for a place I've never been.

—**James Wade**, award-winning author of
Beasts of the Earth and *All Things Left Wild*

The Place the Spiders Waved is an exquisitely observed ode to the wonders, dangers, and history of the brush country. A generous, moving memoir-in-verse that startles and illuminates and above all demonstrates a deep reverence for this complicated land. A book

I'll treasure and press into the hands of anyone who asks why I love South Texas.

—**Katie Gutierrez**, best-selling author of
More than You'll Ever Know

What a thrill to come across a talent like Lucy Griffith, who not only speaks the truth of South Texas/brush country/chaparral doggedness with clarity and spot on recognition, but in a manner both evocative and highly authentic. Hearty welcome to the small but burgeoning school of South Texas authenticity and singularity!

—**William Jack Sibley**, author of
Here We Go Loop De Loop

The Place the Spiders Waved

FLOWERSONG
PRESS

poetry by

Lucy Griffith

FLOWERSONG
PRESS

"We travel to ourselves,
when we go to a place where we have lived."

—**Pascal Mercier**

Dedicated to the families that made this childhood possible:

The McNeels
The Leslies
The Langfords
and the Flores Brothers

.

table of contents

MUY BUENA GENTE

THE GHOSTS OF ESPERANZA

The Place the
Spiders Waved

Sobrevivir

Today an abandoned house
    crumbles in the brush at *Esperanza*.
        No more caretakers.
            No more foremen.

A rusty roof of corduroy.
    A gate on one hinge.
        A porch of broken chairs.
        Empty, yet—

stuffed with song.
    A single shoe, collapsed at the heel.
        A rotten backpack.
            A green blanket quilted with burrs.

Names proclaimed on the walls and rafters
    I was here. I walked here.
        I made my way in the dark.
            Near the stove, a list carefully penned.

        1/3/89
        The Castaños
        from Coahuila:
        Nino, Sambo, Aldaco: centro
        Limón, Luís, Kine, Javier, and Martín: barrio
        100% KREYZY. Loco.

I picture them resting in the kitchen with its cracked floor.
    Savoring shade. A roof. Water. A toilet.
        Sharing beans folded in tortillas.
            Napping in the day.

Walking north at night.
    Those Castaños. 100%.

LESSONS FROM
THE THORN SCRUB

Winter Scene

A cold front
sweeps the dust.
Blue northers, we call them.
All the kids line up

on the corral fence to watch.
A cobalt line of bitter bone,
a frigid seam starts
thin on the horizon,

swells to swallow the sky
in gunmetal.
Sends us scrambling for cover
as the wind lashes grit in our eyes,

stings our shins. Like a magic show,
a tablecloth of warmth
whips aside—
the arctic pours in.

The next morning, I wander,
bulked up under all my shirts.
I walk to the corral,
always drawn to the horses.

The wind tickles up their tails
as they wheel and kick.
Steam shoots from their noses—
now they are dragons.

Bandana Song

I am a bandana,
flag of the *vaquero*.

A neckerchief red, blue, maybe black
woven cotton, maybe silk,
I crave grime from honest work.
Supple in my roles.

I am towel, tie, respirator, mask,
sometimes a strainer, sometimes a quirt.
Wrap me round red iron,
I'm ready to brand.

Twist me into rope,
I'll be a pigging string.
I'm just as happy, wet, under a hat—
or over, snug, to fight a wind-blown sting.

I dry sweat, wipe dust-driven tears &
bloody knives. I scour tin cups.
I can blindfold,
becalm a wild-eyed horse.

Then, scrub me clean, hang me on a fence—
I cape the cowboy before the dance.

Another World

Sixty miles south of San Antonio,
small town Charlotte edges Highway 97.
From the way back of our station wagon
I see the hump of the high school gym slide by. Go Trojans!
I smell the enchiladas at Linda's Café and then—
a stripe of highway dives into the scrub,
we're in another world.

Thickets of blackbrush, huisache, whitebrush,
woven with cactus, tasajillo, prickly pear. Lots of pear.
Switchy mesquite, retama, catclaw, guajillo.
Mile after mile, a vast briar patch.
I crawl out the back window,
open the gate to *Esperanza*.
Dry air prickles my nose.

Two more gates
through grey mounds of Zebu bulls
before we park at the ranch house.
Two buildings, two chimneys,
joined by a wraparound screen porch.
Greeted by *Yoo-hoos* and laughter,
we toss pink and plaid cardboard suitcases.

Each kid claims a cot on the porch.
Grownups settle into rooms with doors.
My sisters grab Tiddly Winks, Jacks,
cigar boxes full of arrowheads.
As oldest girl, I have a chore.
Load the watering can at the sink,
kneel and fill rusted tuna fish cans

that cup each leg of our cots.
Small moats deter centipedes and scorpions.
One time a visiting grandchild,
looking for aspirin
found a rattlesnake in the medicine cabinet.
Grampa, there's a snake in here!
Jess appeared with a rifle.

Shot it right there.
We saw the hole.

Night Ride

Roy Boy rides shotgun, he gets the gates and snakes.
I thread my way to the back, settle my skinny behind
on whiskey bottles, bow ties of wire, fence pliers, lariats.

Jess—owner, Jefe, boss, pointed at Roy Boy and me
You two, get in the Scout. Jess, in wrinkled khaki
steeped in cigars, sweat, Old Fitzgerald.

Where we going, Uncle Jess? He grunts,
pumps the pedal to start the Scout. Into the brush
we drive. We bounce. Full dark now.

Road made of rocks. I hold on with both hands.
The headlights make pink tunnels of light.
Three gates later, we jerk to a stop.

There's a terrible stink. Like skunk spray,
doubled. Clack, clack, clack. A wave of javelina
parts around us, canines clattering, oil-black

manes stiff as forests. Forty humps of darkness
flow around the jeep clicking and grunting,
into the scrub, dissolving to shadows.

Then silence. We move on, slower now,
finally crawl up a berm, stop on top.
Lights off, engine off. A spreading sound

soaks the night. We wait. On the horizon,
a glow grows into a full moon.
A lake of birds. *Sandhill Cranes,* murmurs Jess.

Hundreds upon hundreds, filling the lake
from edge to edge—*singing* to each other,
golden in the moon.

At last, *El Jéfe* starts the Scout again
without a word. Back at the ranch house, all still.
The cots on the porch squeak

beneath our dusty bodies. We lie
awake on limp pillows,
dazzled by gatherings of dark and light.

Down the Steps

One time, a pen of baby goats,
    one time, a copper stallion with one eye.
        Each visit,
           a surprise.

Now a swimming hole. Before our arrival
    earth movers shaped a square mound,
        sealed it with cement.
           A hundred-foot sofa pillow with water in the dimple.

In this arid country, wells are deep,
    water boils with friction as it shoots
        from a fat pipe into the "pool."
           We are warned—

has to cool for a week before you can swim.
    Temptation, a whiff of sulphur.
        Steps of railroad ties
           march into the steaming water.

A tower of inner tubes stands ready.
    My little sister takes off,
        hula-hoops a tube around her waist
           stomps down the steps.

She waves me off with a wrist flick signaling
    You're not the boss of me,
        splashes in,
           turns to me, dazed.

Pain swims across her eyes.
    She does a shaky stagger up the steps,
        her legs scalded lobster red,
            her face crumpled.

Just before her panicked wail,
    my heart fastens to hers,
        my arms reach to gather her, as
            my legs begin to burn.

Here, Now

Monarch
      migration king
           wings of bittersweet
    a thousand miles
with no map

Dinner Bell Benediction

All those meals served with a side of resentment—
I get it now, Mama. Feeding a young family three squares
day in day out. Unthanked.
Occasionally brightened by Adele Davis, or
Cooking with Julia.

My father's careless remark on vegetables
Try cooking them next time.
Now I understand
that subsequent month of silent treatment,
Cheerios for dinner.

No wonder you loved *Esperanza,*
dismissed the risks and dangers.
No trips to Handy-Andy, no bags of groceries, no lists, no ice.
Just your leatherette travel case on the porch, cradling
the twins—your Wild Turkey, Daddy's Cutty Sark.

Three times a day
the bell at the ranch kitchen
would ring,
and all would be handled.
Big fat steaks, homemade biscuits,

calabacitas con carne,
potatoes fried in bacon grease,
pitchers of milk from the cooler.
No clean up, no dishes.
Alberto handled it all.

Now I know why
a pale city girl
afraid of snakes and scorpions
found sweet reprieve,
a vacation from herself. Redeemed—

on the wide porch of a brush country ranch.

Comida de Flores

agarita blossom
vanilla bean
minting the wind

adelia   *anacahuita*   *ébano*   *guayacan*

          colibrí buffet

Hung Out to Dry

Behold the flycatchers,
        elegant peachy Scissortails,

flashy Vermilions.
        Behold the border hosting

the gaudy Green Jay,
        the slow waddle of Inca Doves.

Home to thirty-pound Diamondbacks,
        bobcats, badgers, coatimundi.

Gila monsters, horned toads.
        But the bugs—

massive ants, the color of rubies,
        Rhinoceros beetles that loom.

We watch a dung beetle,
        like a man pushing a bus

roll a ball of manure for hours
        straight and steady across the yard.

Until an epic dry spell,
        year after year

no real moisture.
        Then a rain bomb

blows the lid off our gritty world.
        After an all-night storm serenades on tin, I wake

to a dark porch. Sun's up. Still dark?
 I pull on boots from the pile near the door,

step outside real slow.
 Our porch screens carpeted

with spiders. Tarantulas from gutter to ground.
 Hundreds and hundreds, blocking the light.

They are *waving*.
 Each creature stretches
a hairy black leg
 into the breeze,

one by one,
 to dry.

Hora de Siesta

*I don't care if you take a nap, but you better be
quiet enough for ME to!*

—Dottie Leslie

I slip out, careful for once
not to slam the screen door,
wander over to the barn

where the Flores brothers,
Francisco, Antonio, and Salvador,
sit in the shade

on straight-backed chairs
with hide seats.
I slide a sweaty pad off the rack

and crawl onto a saddle to watch each man work.
Salvador soaps his boots. His socks don't match.
Antonio slices strips of rawhide for a rope,

a jig between his knees holds
a knife for a quarter inch cut.
Francisco's hands, tobacco-colored,

textured as a knot of mesquite,
braid "pulls" of white and black horsehair,
nailed to the porch post.

¿Porqué blanco y negro, Francisco? I ask.
¡Como víbora de cascabel, es buena suerte!
Of course, good luck with rattlers.

As he shares stories with his brothers,
Francisco hitches, without looking.
A skill passed down from Spanish Moors.

Half an inch of weaving takes an hour.
Spellbound, I watch
a bridle grow from a man's hands.

Un Buen Reata

One night, we circle the yard at dusk.
Francisco, Salvador and Antonio stroll from the barn
leading a line-back dun with a fancy saddle.
They wear shiny satin bandanas.
Each cowboy swings a rawhide rope.

First they throw small loops,
snare our ankles as we race the yard like maverick calves.
Then middle-sized loops, figure eights, right, left.
Now man-sized loops, the rope hums.
Antonio steps in and out of a circle

he spins just above the ground,
dancing with the rope.
Slender Francisco jumps the hoop
as he passes the loop
from six feet on one side

to six feet on the other.
For the finale,
Salvador mounts the dun,
stands on the saddle,
Plays out a loop above his head.

His arm swings wide,
the horse still as stone.
The loop sings as it grows,
larger, larger,
until man and horse are circled

by a rope
spinning inches above the ground.
We cheer. We practice our *gritos,*
aye, aye aye.
If there's a cowboy heaven

I like to think there's a dusty circle there,
where the Flores boys
can ease out a rawhide loop,
throw a new trick to
surprise God.

Harder than it looks

Beside a row of upturned saddles
coils a whip for each *vaquero*,

rawhide brown and tan, tripled plaited,
woven on hot afternoons,

hours of braiding,
handles smoothed with use.

I think *how hard could it be?*
I've watched the Flores brothers crack the cattle

forward, an explosion of sound
sprung from their arms.

Just like Antonio,
I swing the bull whip over my head

watch the thong swell before me
in a fetching loop,

snap my wrist,
expertly—clip my ear.

Like a torn shirt,
I wear the humiliation for days.

Self-efficacy

Under the thin shade of *retama*
and salt cedar, the Flores brothers
have split brush, gathered yearlings
into a corral, mesquite limbs
stacked and woven. The bawling

roars. Jess climbs narrow steps
to a stool above a sorting station.
Usually there's a tall handle,
but it's gone. He swings the gate
with his boot, deft as forked lightning,

to shift the cows into three pens.
I perch on the fence rail, studying.
Pretty soon I see the score,
which to keep, which to sell,
which suffer from worms.

He looks over at me.
Wanna try?
Yes, sir.
I climb up and sit beside him.
As the yearlings pass below,

I check for stockiness, scrawniness,
clouds of flies. I proclaim—
Keep. Keep. Sell. Keep. Doctor.
Now I know what to save,
what to let go. And when I call it,

my voice is loud.

Cadillac

The Scout's in use somewhere,
so we get in a dusty, no color Cadillac,

the go-to-town car. Rust streaks
the sides, long scratches, no mirrors.

Uncle Jess, why do you have
a Cadillac on a ranch?

Only car feels right—like a saddle.
We drive in silence, windows open, my braids fly.

I smell sweet blooms of guajillo,
soon erased by columns of dust.

MUY BUENA GENTE

A Gentleman on Horseback

Vaqueros of the brush country are alert, resourceful,
close observers of nature, experts in animal psychology,
possessing a depth of willpower unfamiliar to most men.

— J. Frank Dobie

On the Cassin Ranch in Batesville, Texas
21-year-old Ed sits at the kitchen table.
It's a July afternoon.
He's on his fifth cup of coffee,
eating a bowl of beans
that's been on the back of the stove for a week.

The wall phone rings.
Cassin? Yes, sir.
Jess McNeel. Yes, sir.
My braceros are getting their paperwork sorted in Mexico.
I need some wild cows gathered, 'bout 60 of them.
I hear you're "muy perrito," a good tracker with those ladinos.

Yes, sir. Happy to do it. How about this fall when it's cooler?
They'll die if you work 'em in this heat.
Needs to be done now, got a purebred herd coming in, can't mix 'em.
I can be there tomorrow, sir, but can't make any promises
on their well-being.
Just do what you can. Watch those mossy horns, they'll crawl right up
your rope.
Yes, sir, I know it.

In a week it's done.
Deft with a lariat,

32

partnered with a horse
who can smell a cow in a thicket,
Ed has those wild rangy ones
gathered in a pen, ready to ship.

He leans against his truck, tall,
skinny as a limb of mesquite,
as Jess arrives in his scratched Cadillac.
　　　　Got 60, sir, but one died in the heat.
Jess peels off bills from a fat roll.
Ed takes the cash but pulls a check from his pocket.

What's this?
　　　　Paying up on the dead cow, sir. I'm mighty sorry.
Oh hell, son. Jess tears up the check—
pieces scatter in the wind.

Flycatcher Song

Taloned upon
Spanish Dagger, a
vermillion puff ball,
the flycatcher

leans into a blue norther—
a gaudy ornament.
Yucca point, beak point,
feather point, claw.

Pom-pom, scarlet fluff,
half an ounce of clinging duff.
Angling in, pressed against the wind
like a long kiss.

In this scene of
crimson and green,
he etches the lesson.
When you're trapped in a gale,

befriend the wind.

Breakfast in Winter

At one end of the horse corral,
Francisco balances on the end of a railroad car,
his bandana warms his face.
To feed molasses,

he spins a valve
at the end of the car.
Glugging out, plop, plop,
black mayonnaise.

My dragons dive into the trough,
slurp, lick, then return,
sticky, to their hay.
Their muzzles prickle up like porcupines.

Lessons of the Lazy Susan

The Pied Piper smell   of homemade tortillas lures me
off the sleeping porch before light. I run across the yard to the
stucco building. Just outside hangs a dinner bell with a horsehair
pull next to a long sink for handwashing. I slip in,   curl in a
chair by the door, high-backed and cupped like a palm. I sit with
my knees up,   watch the cook.

Alberto, famous for being able to tame a wild cow to milk—in
just one day. He'd have his head in her flank in no time,
singing to her. Alberto's shiny already from scratch baking, his
flour-sack apron marked with effort. In front of the wide stove,
shimmering with heat is a wide round table. On it is a Lazy Susan
big as the wagon wheel light hung above. A carousel of bounty.

Tortillas overflow a basket.   Biscuits, big as a fist, are stacked
next to a sticky quart of honey,
another jet black with molasses. A coke bottle, corked, holds oil
and vinegar, tinted orange with *chili pequins*. There's a mountain
          of bacon, a platter of sausage patties, a yellow bowl of
huevos revueltos, an *olla* of frijoles,   fragrant with *epazote*.

Alberto slips me a tortilla, smeared with refried beans. The
braceros trickle in, shaking water from their hands, grab tin plates
speckled with enamel. The screen door slams.
From behind my knees, I watch, listen,   practice my
Spanish.   They talk of horses and ropes.

Mostly they tease, especially Alberto.
Call him *Mujer, Conejo*.

It makes me mad.

Alberto just keeps bringing food.
He smiles at second helpings.

Lazy Susan keeps cruising,
never still, never still.

Now, decades later,
I am the cook for the crowd.

I apply the lessons of the Lazy Susan.

> Use plates that won't break.
> Some will want it hot.
> Some will want it sweet.
> Set food in the middle and easy to get.
> Plenty is better than fancy.
> Always put something special in your beans.

Kids

As oldest girl, I lead.
Near the camp kitchen
we tumble over a mesquite fence
into a pen of Spanish goats,
brown, black,
speckled, splashed.

In the smell and feel of them,
we pet their milk bellies, brush,
fashion halters of scrap rope,
weave dry grasses into sparse manes.
Their cries, human.
Pellets tumble from under their tails.

We name them to claim them,
Brownie, Fury,
Spot, Frisco.
Arms and laps
cradle warm bodies,
Hands shine with lanolin.

Sunday morning
we find the pen half-empty.
Alberto, the cook, stands inside
over an enamel pan
with a blue rim,
his apron bloody red.

In unison we scream "No!"
He laughs, his gold tooth winks
as he grabs a goat, knife shiny,

quickly swipes across the throat,
a dark ribbon, a shuttered cry,
a gout of gore,

laughs again.
¡Cabrito! Barbacoa!
I gather my troops,
climb the fence,
wipe tears.
Propose a hunger strike.

Tough Truth

When we complained to Jess about the
fate of baby goats, he was stern—
It's a ranch,
know where your food comes from.

Our milk weighed down a pitcher
in the cooler
milked that morning,
Alberto's first chore.

Our steaks cut from a steer
that had eaten prickly pear the day before.
Calabacitas hung, green-striped, on the yard fence,
chili pequins twinkled crimson in the shade.

I remember that now,
I remember, *It's a ranch*
when processing a deer
or carving a wild hog into hams

or canning tomatoes from my garden.
Thrilling to the thrust of first asparagus.
Six weeks
of tender tips ahead.

Panzón lleno, corazón contento

Laced with recurved prickles
from November through April—
tiny white blossoms of guajillo bush
carpet the ranch, sugar the air.

Filling caves and hollow trees,
honey from guajillo
won the blue ribbon in Paris
at the 1900 World's Fair.

Dark amber, runny, not too sweet,
a touch of earth on the tongue.
According to legend,
well-drillers slid

through thirty feet
of comb and honey
on their way through
earth to water.

Each year scores of white hives
tucked in the brush fill
60 half-gallon silvery paint cans
that leave tawny circles

on pantry shelves and Lazy Susans.
I can still see us around the table, all the kids—
faces and fingers sticky,
crumbs on our chins,

savoring the marriage of guajillo honey
to Alberto's cornbread. Reverent,
we learn the meaning of
panzón lleno, corazón contento.

Into the Mogote

One summer, *El Jéfe* buys an entire railcar
of small horses, breed name—
Pony of the Americas.
The name thrilled me.
The Flores brothers gentle them before our arrival.
Line them up on the yard fence, large to small.

To twelve-year-old eyes,
everything Esperanza seems oversized—
snakes that drape the width of the road,
bulldozers that clatter all night,
a Zebu bull as tall as a truck,
molasses delivered in a train car.

A few sorrels with flaxen manes,
but most mottled gray.
We saddle up, head out the gate. From above,
we look like desert raiders,
trailing wild curves of dust.
I lead through the blackjack and guajillo, the *mogote.*

Splitting the brush, just like the *vaqueros.*
The youngest brings up the rear on the smallest pony.
He grips the saddle horn with both hands, eyes wide.
We trot the sandy parts, walk the rough.
The ponies short legs jiggle our bones.
I hear the kids giggling behind me.

We're a posse now,
hunting bandits, free from adults,
on our dappled ponies
in the dappled shade.

Concentrate

'til by turning, turning, we come out right.

—Joseph Brackett

As a child, Esperanza seemed the end of something,
boundary-less, fences incidental.
I remember thinking
about Mexico nearby.

The space between the thickets called a *sendero*,
a wide path I follow into the labyrinth,
remembering always to turn one way, this is no place to get lost.
Senderos curve into
interlocking warrens of dangers,

fence builders boasted of 23 rattlesnakes
in less than a hundred yards.

Careful is a rule, not an option,
woven into the *mogote*. Watch each step.
Look up, the only horizon—brush and pear
over your head.
At night a strong darkness,
you could hear it breathing.
A concentrate of sounds, thick as syrup.

Once a wild bull in
a pen made of pipes
crashed all night.
Rage with four legs.

A Day's Work

—for David Langford

4 a.m., you head for the barn, carry
cubes of beef tucked in biscuits,

bound tight in a bandana.
In the moonlight,

a loop flies across the corral,
lassoes a mount from the *remuda*.

The percussion of hoofbeats,
muscled shoulders slap against one another,

then quiet.
Two *vaqueros*

saddle up in the dark, saddle by feel.
Each step a muscle memory.

Two always
for safety in forty square miles

of brush country.
By sunup, you make it to the

farthest pasture,
grab a drink at the windmill,

a tin cup swings from baling wire.
Now, the chore.

Doctor, worm, brand or count.
Trot home, arrive

in the sandy dusk.
Drink, eat, shower.

El Jéfe strolls to the bunkhouse.
Well, men, it's cooled off.

Let's go pull that windmill.
We'll be done by midnight, for sure!

Rough Country

In the brush country, gear
tells a story.

Saddles look like they've been drug behind a truck
for a mile or ten.

Tapaderos over the stirrups
rubbed of their color. Leather polished thin.

At Esperanza each *vaquero* had
a little pocket hung from the pommel,

sticky with screwworm dope.
Now sized for cell phones.

In easy reach,
a rifle scabbard angled under the left fender.

Usually a .30-.30 Model 94, lever action.
Ready for snakes, ready for rabbit stew.

Those .30-.30s are still around.
I saw one leaning near the front door

of a ranch in Batesville.
A third of the walnut stock gone.

Sir, I believe the rats have gotten to your rifle.
Maybe we should hang it up?

Naw. No rats. Riding in the brush.

Pila

As the *papalote*
spins in the wind,
the sucker-rod strides up and down,
carousel style, pushing
arterial squirts into

troughs of stone, steel, concrete,
one hollowed out of an old mesquite.
Trough, tank, water hole, *pila*.
A heartbeat at the hub of spoked paths—
water makes community.

I scoop a warm hatful from the *pila*,
slip beneath a *palo verde*
to sit cross-legged.
Polywog, mosquito,
damselfly and dragon throb the surface.

I watch and drip,
wait for more visitors.
Butterfly, bee, and rusty wasp.
A mirror of blue sky
hung with jewels,

Painted Bunting
with *siete colores,*
Green Jay, Vermillion Flycatcher
adorn the edge, dipping
rhythmically as child's toys.

Cattle, horses bury their noses twice a day,
nudging waves that overflow to splash speckled frogs.
Mule deer, coyote,
bobcat lap in the dark with
javelina and raccoon.

The pulse of *Esperanza* beats in scattered pools.

Prickly Opulence

Witness my finery. Vipers tangle my hair,
scorpions dangle from my ears,
centipedes bracelet my wrists.

I've been marked. Santa Anna's army
left its wide furrow across my belly.
I've been root-plowed, deep-drilled.

Boars wallow in my secrets
fat on the beans of mesquite.
The drier the spring, the stouter the bean.

But each April, I flower—
balsam-breathed with *guajillo*
I make a fog of honey.

My charms are subtle
a smell, a surprise,
the wolf-whistle of *pauraque.*

I am *Esperanza,* named for hope.
Always hope for rain.
I persevere.

The Dope Bucket

Flesh-munching maggots,
they can burrow two inches,

eat a cow, horse, goat,
pig, or deer alive.

Screw worms mean weekly checks.
A good dog can smell them,

a good dog won't ever bite, make
more holes to doctor.

Ears flicking, tail wringing,
sure signs of a wormy cow.

In a horn wound or ear mark—
screw worms drive cows crazy.

Wheeling and head tossing,
they try to run away from themselves.

The Flores brothers gather them
to the pens, rope them quietly,

hold each one down for doctoring.
Eleven and spry, I get to run the "Dope Bucket."

Two Folgers cans wired together
with a handle in the middle,

a paint brush stuck in each can.
On one side yellowish linseed oil

splashing and daubing a still-smoking brand.
El Jéfe says, *Dope it good,*

You've got the most important job
at Esperanza right now.

In the other can, Smear 62,
thick, oily reddish-black.

Burns on contact,
keeps on burning. Smells like poison.

62 is for lobbing big gobs
in wormy castration cuts,

the hole where a horn was removed.
Big gobs. Maggots come writhing out,

screwing themselves out of
wet hidden warmth.

My eyes water.
My hands burn.

I am Master of the Plague.
Holes grow in my shirt.

Rolling the Rowel

The spur of the *vaquero*
is a signature.
A tool to fit boot and body,
a second pair of hands,

a set of old friends, company at work.
The spurs of the Flores brothers
project their personalities—
Salvador's cloverleaf rowels,

so mild, so rarely applied,
a simple S stamped on the shank.
First, he points the horse
with a twist of his head,

then a touch of his calf,
only then—a roll of the rowel.
A messaging trick.
Salvador, master of

see how little it takes.
Francisco and Antonio sport worn
12-tine rowels on a straight shaft,
weathered chap guards,

polished by brush and thorns.
Rowels to nudge, not gouge.
Simple silver shapes hint at a windmill,
with rowels for blades.

All the silver they own—close to the horse.
Quiet men, straightforward tastes.
No showy jingling.
Talents do the talking.

Cuentos de Papalote

Planted sturdy in the scrub,
as watchtower of the wind, I stand.
My vane yields to breeze,
my meetings—all face to face.

As my sister, Singer,
lifts a thread,
I am Aero—
lifting water with my broken sail.

Grayed by many weathers,
I gather and give their tales,
easterlies spiked with brine—
swells of wet,

the twisted spawn of hurricanes.
Pierced by lightning,
parched by the scirocco of westerlies,
I am woven tight with heat.

When days are short,
the seam of a blue norther
rolls over my thickets, in an hour
turns sweat to snow.

Steady as a heartbeat,
I mill the wind for water.
Up, down,
stitching weft and woof.

Sheltered

At *Esperanza*, two modest houses
20 feet apart are surrounded,
like a bear hug,
with a screened porch.

The space between
a roomy dogtrot that
funnels any breeze—
a taste from Aransas Bay, heavy, salty,

or one honeyed with fruit blossoms, spring
gifts from orchards in the Valley.
Visiting kids *owned* the porch, framed by a
massive fan on one end, tall as a man,

hammocks on the other.
A trio of tricycles
nosed in the corner
like ponies at their hay.

Some hidden instinct
from our ancients?
What hardwires us to crave
an outlook, sheltered?

A row of metal cots, draped in old quilts.
Pick-up-sticks, wooden boxes of arrowheads,
comics line low shelves.
Small chairs from Mexico

harbor us for an afternoon read.

They look like leather drums,
smell like the tack room. We watch
hummers mob the feeders under the eaves.

Outside, inside.
Untamed, contained.
When there's trouble in the world
and you wonder where I am—

I'll be on the porch.

Busted Fence Tryptic

on strands of barbed wire   parades a buffet

skewered by a shrike   lizard wasp frog

oysters from   calves   no longer
                                                          toros

pear burners toast   quick *comida buena*   what tough
creatures

tore through this fence   a tangle now to untangle   this
                                                         vaquero afternoon

Barbed Remarks from the Shrikes

You see medieval heads on pikes,
a thorny tree of pain, call us Butcher Bird.

Don't taint us with your war metaphors.
We are handsome Zorros,

hovering
with masks and capes of grey,

dapper
pleated handkerchiefs tucked in our wings.

Within the cage of our ribs
beats the heart of an eagle.

Our toothed beaks
tote lizard beetle chickadee wasp

to our spiny home.
Hanging meat to cure to rawhide,

those dried kabobs
get us through droughts,

feed us in the cold.
Welcome to our pantry, well-stocked.

Ballad of Big Ears

So hot.
Everyone's asleep.
I slide out the porch door,
open the gate,
remember to look for snakes.

Wander down the *sendero*—
borrow shade
from a twisted mesquite.
Sit in the sand and watch.
A shape of jackrabbit

lifts from tawny scrub.
She knows I'm here,
flattens radar ears along her back,
pretends to disappear.
Her ticked fur ripples

with quick breaths.
Soon, she relaxes, her ears lift.
So thin I see a delta of red vessels.
Ears as cooling towers, shedding heat.
She must have parked on an ant mound.

She somersaults over my head,
shudders them off.
From this moment,
a lifetime fondness.
Those "listeners."

Burros, Bassets and
Bloodhounds,
bats, foxes,
a boy with freckles
who calls me "Teach."

Sky Dance

Wheeling black confetti,
    against a dusky sky,
        bats scoop up our bugs.

Their orbits weave,
punctuating our eventide
        with arabesques and pirouettes.

Tiny mammals, sky pups,
    their cave upended,
        until the dawn's return.

THE GHOSTS OF ESPERANZA

Before the Seventh Flag Flew Over Texas

Before the sooty flags of gas flares,
before the rhythm of pump jacks
pecking at her skin,
before gates
that swing
at the push of a button,

before Texas,
before slavery in Mexico's silver mines,
before smallpox,
before the Spaniards,
their policy of *"reducción,"*
before the shattering—

First Nation
indigenous peoples,
bands of Coahuiltecan,
Comecrudo—Cotoname—Carrizo—Pakawa—Payaya
follow food and rain
across the flanks of Esperanza.

In summer,
prickly pear pads and violet fruits,
bulbs of sotol
roasted underground,
beans of mesquite
ground for flour.

In autumn, pecans.
In a wet year,
a shaggy bison
wandering south.
Always lizards, ants and seeds.
You stalk thunderstorms and ripened fruit,

travel from camp to camp,
circular shelters of four bent poles, woven nets.
In gratitude for food
you dance all night—a *mitotique*
spiced with *peyote*
on the banks of a creek called Hope.

Raven Evermore

You can tell how long we've paired
by how we fly, you and I—

rowing past in tandem, blacker than black
then twisting to flash, silvered with sun. Soft muttering,

turning in concert. I know your moves.
I've preened every feather, those small ones round your eyes.

The longer our bond the more perfect
our sky ballet, inches apart,

monogamy made synchrony. Climbing into clouds,
wing-folding into steep stoop, air-dancing,

falling together to pull a sweet glide.
Our world in each other, safe and rich.

Fly with me now, wingtip to wingtip
two hearts drumming a single song.

Showing Up

In a backyard in Cotulla one warm night,
Charlie told me stories.
How Jess hired him
to gather some wild cows

at *La Perla* Ranch near the border.
He called Jess *Ol'MACK-neel.*
Dropped Charlie and his best horse, Chapo,
off to get the job done.

Them cows was worse than wild,
they was RANK. One bull
came right up my rope, knocked us over,
broke this leg right here.

Lucky I did just one dally round the saddle horn, or
that bull mighta drug us both to Mexico.
Anyways, Ol' Mack-neel came back
to find me in a right mess.

Drove me to the Laredo hospital.
The doctors set my leg,
cast it,
hung it in a sling over the bed.

I hate being laid up. Makes me cranky.
Mack-neel stayed with me though,
all week.
Snuck in beer and tacos, smoked cigars,

told stories till I got sprung.
Surprising in a boss.
He's ridden some rusty edges himself, I guess.
Never forget it. Ol' Mack-neel.

As for me,
I've spent too much time
in the murk of a hospital alone,
curled on boiled sheets. Weak and dreamy,

wrapping my heart around
babies unable to come to term,

I watched the clock hours
stalk by in stiff boots

until I inhabited a solitude so deep
I thought to change my name.
Now, this I know,
when you find a man, fiercely tender

who would spend the night on a hospital floor
who would keep watch,
when you find a man, who shows up—
rope him good and dally it twice.

Priorities

The man who does not manifest love in the present, has not love.

—Tolstoy

Even as a child
I saw the melancholy in the man.
Fierce opinions, too,
but Jess wore sadness in repose.

Perhaps having a Texas Ranger as a dad
forged you,
or maybe that time you ran away on horseback,
returned after three days

unnoticed going, unnoticed returning.
Perhaps that left a hollow space.
So when first wife Adalee, long
sick with cancer

moved to the hospital in San Antonio,
you kept busy at the ranch,
working, working.
until you got a call.

Her time was near.

Frantic, you took off to the barn,
backed out the go-to-town Cadillac.
Three gates between you and the highway,

you busted through them all.

To hell with scattered cattle.
To hell with repair.
Broken headlights,

hub caps rolling into the scrub.

You made it in time to say goodbye,
to say goodbye,
goodbye with gate-busting love.

What Happened

In a backyard in Cotulla on an evening in spring,   my
favorite seat—between the Boeker brothers. In their eighties,
with fine straw hats, faces carved from long days in the saddle,
I sit between Ralph and Charlie,   in mostly white
plastic chairs sharing fried catfish, fried everything really, and
stories of the border. I find out   how lucky I was, and
what happened.

> *Did you know those Flores brothers*
> *were probably the best cowboys in the whole state?*
>
> *Whatever jackpot rodeo they picked, they won.*
> *Sent all the money home to Mexico.*

Ralph, what happened to the Flores brothers?

> *On the way to Eagle Pass, their truck flipped.*
> *Kilt them all. That was a bad day.*

The Real Thing

Ed Cassin died at his South Texas Ranch at the age of 93

Makes sense to die out here in the brush. That is good.
I was checking on a mama cow and her calf.
You know, those French cows are terrible mothers.

They're white and pretty though. Weigh out good.
I like the Bremmers for mama cows.
Real careful with their babies.

This is where I've always belonged.
I only lasted a few days at A&M, got so homesick.
Different kind of learning suits me.

Which horse is best for branding.
Which one to saddle to find wily steers.
How to make a pot of beans last a week.
How to be alone for months at a time.
How to walk away when a man's made a right fool of himself.
Why I depend on handshake deals.
How to smile when a greenhorn tells you how it should be done.
And 'specially, how to find an old flame and rope her back in.

I've had a grand life.
You can too.
Follow these rules.

Sleep outside whenever you can.
When you have thieving rights, share your bounty.
Have a backup hat that's all broke in.
Take off your "spoirs" before you drive, it draws unwanted attention.
And when the road gets muddy—*floor* it.

'Buela Days

Ursula, Patron Saint of Orphans and
Agatha, Benefactor to Bakers.
In my world, *Esperanza,*
Patron Saint of Memorable Childhoods.

Her reservoir of experiences
lives on in my granddaughters.

They call me 'Buela
and feel the touch of *Esperanza*
at each visit.
No TV. No phones. No games.

Long walks in the pasture with me,
in all weathers.
Foggy explorations of spider webs,
feeling the ribbon candy of

Frostweed sap after a blue norther.
Watching fingernail-sized blond frogs
bounce at the pond,
spying the snapping turtle.

After I've given two warnings,
Esperanza intercedes—
then lets the fire ants,
cactus needles or slippery rocks teach the lesson.

Esperanza must smile
when their pockets
are lumpy with worked chert,
or writhe with fat grasshoppers, *one of each color!*

When a three-year-old bellows, *Mouse,*
from her highchair by the birdfeeder,
naming the Black-crested Titmouse
as it nabs a sunflower seed.

At the altar of *Esperanza*
lives a pile of deer bones and seed pods,
river rocks painted into carrots and apples,
memories of owl calls, the squelch of tree frogs, shooting stars.

Coyote Call

I sail on a ship of desert sky

      the flute of your starlit song

            trots the beams of my ribs

A Fair Cut

From the walk-in cooler
floats a watermelon, green striped,

a royal Queen of Summer.
Jess produces a sharp blade—

cuts lengthwise,
no O-rings, no semi-circles,

No, this way,
the Mexican way is more fair.

Each of us bestowed a lengthy slice,
a trough of melon,

we bury our chins, a wedge so long
we must balance on our knees.

We spit seeds. A sticky scene.
All are granted some sugary heart.

Ghost Sonata

The ghost strides through camp
rustling a long denim skirt, concho belt swinging,
hat with a wide brim.

She pulls the bell for dinner,
ensures there's plenty, wanders out back,
checks the pit fire.

No wind, no cinders. Good.
          For work, she is armored—
leggings, bandana, gauntleted gloves.

She sings in Spanish,
whispers to horses,
                reads the weather with her nose.

Crescendos with attention.
          She is an anthem to wilderness,
thorn and barb ten feet high.

a barrier of jimco, blue-berried coma,
wands of retama, spiny mesquite.
She croons a lullaby,

sandhill cranes bugling overhead
          in skeins of peach and gray. You hear her in
                flock after flock of geese rafting to Mexico.

Her drumbeat is the
syncopated crackle
of a buck fight,

the sharp retort of antler strikes,
        the soft bell of milkcow, the
tincup against the windmill.

Kaleidoscope

Lemony plankton in the wind,
      a thousand sulfur butterflies ride the trades.

Cliff swallows—
      seals of the sky,

swim against the tide,
      gulping bits of gold.

Jaguar

{Ex-tir-pate: v. root out and destroy completely,
in a particular area}

As late as the 30's
you roamed the *Esperanza.*
The largest cat in North America,
you made a diet of javelina and deer,

the occasional careless bear,
until a trapper tricked you gone
with a smelly bait, hiding a
carbon atom triple-bonded to nitrogen,

cyanide to end your reign.

*Yaguaret*é, the true cat
who loves to swim and fish.
Who knows when to be seen
and when not.

Who lives and hunts alone.
Symbol of vision,
prescience, confidence.
Legend says you shape-shift.

Into the scrub at dusk,
I walk with your ghost—
fit my prints into yours,
your dark coat ripples,

your muscles slide beneath my skin,
my nose lifts to read the air.
I climb into gnarled mesquite,
shape my body along a limb.

I am not destroyed.
I am breathing,
in and out,
breathing in the trees.

The Hand of *Esperanza*

tracks flour on my belly
from a cloud of scratch biscuits.

She wraps her wiry fingers through mine,
to christen a ranch brand,

smoke and sizzle on a rough-hewn bench.
I feel her grip my shoulder—

Just wait…listen to
that sound in the brush.

Esperanza points to bones, arrowheads
that make my granddaughter gasp.

Her spoon stirs the smell of a mesquite fire,
the burble of beans cooked outside.

Her hand guides my knife to dress out a deer,
cook for 15, collect baskets, quilts crafted by hand.

The hand of Esperanza supports the small of my back
when I show up for a sick friend,

when I teach how to look at hard things.
I hear her whisper

You are not your pain,
then feel her cuff my shoulder—

get outside now, go hunting.
Stalk the wisdom of the wild.

El Tuerto

Francisco says the stallion lost an eye
tossing his head, hitting a nail.
One side now gone from sight.
When I ask why they keep him,
Francisco gestures

to a pasture of coppery yearlings—
Todavía esta bueno en su trabajo.
Yes, still good at his job.
I return after the ranch is quiet.
I make myself look.

One warm brown eye,
one sunken, empty, red, and weeping.
I sit on the fence rail, talk to *Tuerto.*
Soon, he comes to me.
I blow in his nostrils like the Comanches

so he will know me forever.
Each day I visit and we talk.
I dip a hand in molasses, let him lick
with the wet velvet of his tongue.
Finally, I find an old diaper, soak it in the trough.

Slow. Slow. I stroke his blind side.
Easy now, *tranquilo, Tuerto.*
I wipe his eye,
banish the gnats,
clean the path of tears.

He leans his head against my chest.

Demasiado

Late July afternoon at the corrals
I sense something wrong.
      I'm good at that.

Absent, the usual laughing singing teasing.
The *vaqueros* are back from branding,
      but it's too quiet.

I spy a red mare alone in a pen,
head down, nose almost to the ground.
      It's hot, still she trembles in a long quaver.

Next morning, I'm up early to check on her—
gone. Out in the brush I see a red hump—
      three vultures lined up on the hill of her.

I ask Salvador
¿Que pasó a la yegua?
      He replies *El hombre nuevo montó hasta la muerte.*

Shakes his head, disgusted with the new hire
a vaquero knows better
      Macho, he spits.

Thirty horses in the *remuda,*
plenty to trade out or just slow down.
      Heat means rest.

Ridden to death.
I go through the gate to her,
      shoo away the vultures with a *grito* and a stomp.

Pick some dead grasses,
gather straggly flowers,
     lay them by.

Shaped in the Thorn Scrub

The chain lightning of memory and family never quits in us.

—Ivan Doig

At the intersection of landscape and character
I look both ways and wonder—
who raised me?

Gentle-voiced Maria,
who crooned my first word, *jugo,*
installed a passion for the smell of damp *masa* on a *comal.*

Or my father?
Who taught me to carve, to hammer,
to drive a tractor, to name each bird.

The auntie who told my mother—
"Laura Jane, let her go, she'll be fine."
who threw open the gate for my wanderings.

Perhaps it was *Esperanza* who raised me.
The brush country filled those gaps in the shape of myself
with lessons in thorn and fang.

Watch where you step.
Maimed is not dead. Horses are teachers.
Calm the little ones.

I did grow up on *Esperanza.*
I am there still, standing
at the corner of Prickly Pear and Briar.

Reverie

In my heaven
there's a field
of windmill grass,

fringed in blackbrush,
towers of prickly pear,
their violet fruits aflame.

A herd of Zebu grazes the edges,
one mama as sentinel
over a puppy pile of calves.

A pond of dove-grays,
slick coats,
pendulous ears.

They float in a tangle of
soft shoulders,
bellies full of milk.

Lean lanolin necks,
lashes of absurd lengths,
damp muzzles, a peaceful commune.

Each calf a pillow,
they rest against each other
breathing in the sun.

When I die,
I want to come back as a Zebu calf.
I'll be the one in the middle.

In Gratitude

My deepest thanks go to the family, friends, mentors and departeds for whom these poems were written. I am grateful for your wisdom, your generosity and your memories. In particular, Laura Georgakakos' enthusiasm for this project kept it simmering until this stew of recollections was tender and table-ready.

In addition, I am so grateful to Myrna and David Langford and Sharron and Larry Jay for reintroducing me to long-ago places which amplified so many memories. My sisters, Becky Fowlkes and Lellen Lane, supported me at every turn.

Heartfelt thanks to Mike Capron whose art and sketches add so much life to my poems. Your love and respect for the brush country is inspiring and your bigheartedness moves me to tears.

I am forever indebted to Edward Vidaurre, the publisher of FlowerSong Press who believed in this love letter to the brush country and made it possible to get it out in the world.

No poet goes it alone and I am lucky to have poets around me who read and reflected on these poems as they developed. Thank you to Athena Kildegaard for her sturdy belief in my work, to Tyler Mills for helping to shape and refine this story, to Scott Stubbs, Lee Robinson and Judith Youngers for braving so many early drafts. Naomi Shihab Nye has championed this project with her advice and fierce enthusiasm. I'd be lost without all of you.

I consider myself lucky beyond measure to know author James Wade, whose friendship and community building has changed and buoyed me. I am steadied by his regard and encouragement of my work.

Finally, and always, thank you to my love Andrew Robinson, my staunchest supporter, always there to encourage me. If I had come with an operating manual, you would have written it.

Acknowledgments

Grateful acknowledgment is made to the editors of the following anthologies and journals, in which these poems were first curated, sometimes in slightly different versions.

- *San Pedro River Review:*
  "*Demasiado,*" nominated for a Pushcart Prize, "Down the Steps," "Dinner Bell Benediction"

- *Texas Observer:*
  "*Sobrevivir,*" April/May 2021

- *Southwestern American Literature:*
  "*Buen Reata,*" "Ghost Sonata," "Priorities"

- *Iron Horse Literary Review, Power Issue:*
  "Winter Scene"

- *Sow's Ear Poetry Review:*
  "Self-efficacy," "Night Ride"

- *Cholla Needles Poetry Magazine:*
  "Hung Out to Dry," "*Comida de flores,*" "The Hand of Esperanza," "*Cuentos de Papalote,*" "Coyote Call," "Ballad of Big Ears," "Harder than it Looks"

About the Author

Lucy Griffith lives beside the Guadalupe River near Comfort, Texas. As a retired psychologist, she explored the imagined life of the Burro Lady of West Texas in her debut collection, *We Make a Tiny Herd,* earning both the Wrangler and Willa Prizes. Her second collection, *Wingbeat Atlas,* pairs her poems with images by wildlife photographer Ken Butler, to celebrate our citizens of the sky.

FLOWERSONG
PRESS

FlowerSong Press nurtures essential verse from, about, and throughout the borderlands. Literary. Lyrical. Boundless.

Sign up for announcements about
new and upcoming titles at:

www.flowersongpress.com